Achievement Journal

You Are More Than Enough

This journal belongs to:

Name _____

Address _____

_____

Phone_____

E-mail _____

Achievement Journal

You Are More Than Enough

Stephens Press · Las Vegas, Nevada

Art Direction: Sue Campbell
Design: Judi Moreo
Affirmations: Charlotte Foust

ISBN 10: 1-932173-65-X
ISBN 13: 9781-932173-659

STEPHENS PRESS, LLC
A Stephens Media Company

Post Office Box 1600
Las Vegas, NV 89125-1600
www.stephenspress.com

Printed in Hong Kong

What People Are Saying

"Judi Moreo has been my business partner in Turning Point International since 1993. We co-founded our business as a direct result of the goals we had set the previous year. We have made it a habit to take magazines, scissors and glue and spend time cutting and pasting our pictures and words from these magazines of everything we wanted to do, to be and to have for the coming year. Usually, before even half of the year was through—we had accomplished most of our goals! It was during one of these times we decided to go one step further and we created a goal *Achievement Journal* for our business. I know from first hand experience that the *Achievement Journal* works because my goals always become my reality just by using it! Anyone that has dreams and doesn't know how to take the right steps can propel their lives forward into having more than they can ever have imagined so easily by using Judi's *Achievement Journal*."

— FIONA CARMICHAEL
MOTIVATIONAL SPEAKER

"Judi Moreo first introduced me to her Goal Achievement Method of setting goals over 15 years ago and I have been using it ever since. It helps me clarify my intentions so that my goals are what I truly want instead of what I think I should do based on family/societal influences. I've given copies of her journal to all my friends and as a college career advisor I use the principles it contains to help my students."

— SUE BRACKSIECK
EASTERN NEW MEXICO UNIVERSITY

"I attended Judi's 'Communicating with Tact and Finesse' class at Nebraska Department of Roads last year. She mentioned in class we should write our wish list in a book and see if it comes true. I thought this was a long shot, but tried it anyway. I recently ran across the notebook I had written it in and everything in the book came true. Unbelievable! The writing of my wishes/goals will now be a yearly ritual. "

— JILL KUHEL
NEBRASKA DEPARTMENT OF ROADS

"I've set powerful goals with my *Achievement Journal* and achieved my dream of becoming a best selling author."

— GREGORY A. KOMPES
AUTHOR, *50 FABULOUS GAY-FRIENDLY PLACES TO LIVE*

"I have always been a goal achiever, but Judi Moreo's journal has taken my goal achievement to a new level. She has provided a workable structure for setting and achieving goals as well as the tools to help others discover their uniqueness and believe in themselves."

— LYNETTE CHAPPELL
SIEGFRIED & ROY PRODUCTIONS

"My only real goals are the ones I write down and date as to when I want to achieve them. Writing goals in my journal and updating them regularly helps me stay on track. It's about time someone published a convenient, well-organized journal people would really use. I should have known that person would be Judi."

— BOB WALKER
SPEAKER/AUTHOR

Contents

Follow Your Star

To be a star you must
shine your own light,
follow your own path
and don't worry
about the darkness . . .
for that is when
stars shine brightest!

Finding Your Purpose, Passion & Power

This journal was designed by Judi Moreo and Charlotte Foust as a companion to Judi's book, *You Are More than Enough: Every Woman's Guide to Purpose, Passion, and Power.* This journal is a tool for your journey to achievement. It has been designed to assist you in achieving your goals. It is a fast, easy, convenient way to record your wants, hopes, and desires; to write down your ideas; and to create the life that you've dreamed of.

When you write in this journal on a regular basis, it keeps you future-focused toward the achievement of your goals and dreams. By journaling, you have the opportunity to review what you have written, keeping these ideas in the forefront of your imagination.

It will provide you with a record of your strengths and successes as well as an acknowledgement of the characteristics, values, talents, people and things for which you are grateful.

Success is a conscious decision.

Our thoughts determine what we want. Our actions determine what we get. Think what you want and then take action. Your first action is to make your desires specific and visual. The second is to make a conscious decision and a plan to get what you want. Don't let fear or negative self-talk hold you back.

When you want something better, you have to do something different than you are doing now. Make the decision that you will be successful and know that you have the power to create whatever success you want in your life. Then, start to take steps in the direction that you want to go.

You can achieve whatever you want to achieve. You are more than enough!

How to use this journal

Express yourself freely in this journal. It is yours. It is not for you to share with anyone else. It is for you to express your desires, interests, and passions. It's time to release your limitations.

You are not to write anything negative in this journal. It is a tool for you to create the future, not dredge up the unwanted past. There is, of course, a place for you to record your successes, so that you can review them and remind yourself of your achievements.

The time to begin is now! It doesn't matter whether it's Monday or Wednesday, January or July, the first or the twenty-first, today is the day to begin your journey. Don't wait for the "right" time or "next month" or "in the morning." Now is the right time to begin. Every twenty-one days, you will have the opportunity to reflect on your accomplishments and plan the next step in your journey. This is your journey. It's ok not to write every day. It's ok not to fill each day. It's also ok to write more than will fit on just one day. If you skip a day, simply pick up where you left off in the next available space. If you date your entries, you will have a way to track your personal time table against the calendar. We all march to a different beat. Every day, week, month and year that you keep your journal becomes easier and more fulfilling.

Charting your course

On the following pages, you will find instructions and samples for completing the different types of pages in the journal. Each of the pages is designed to help you set your vision, define your goals, clarify your dreams and plan the actions it will take to move you toward the fulfillment of your desires and the rich, full life you deserve.

Acknowledge and reward your progress

When you finish a project, reach a goal or stay on your diet one more day, give yourself recognition in your journal. There are many kinds of stickers available. You can use gold stars or stickers that say "Atta Boy!" "Great Job!" or "Wow!" Make sure you have a generous supply of the ones that make you feel good about yourself. Included in your journal is a page of gold stars to start you off. Put the stars and stickers in your journal, your day planner, and anywhere else that will remind you of your successes.

I think I can . . . so I will.

In the Beginning

As you begin planning where you are going, it is wise to determine your starting point. You take a different road to New York when you leave from Orlando than when you leave from Los Angeles. Spend some time with yourself and begin the process of "Realizing Who You Are." Explore the possibilities and imagine you are already there. Ask yourself the questions that are listed on these pages and write your answers. Be honest with yourself — not critical. Remember, this journal is a

Realize Who You Are

> All the world is a stage, And all the men and women merely players. They have their exits and entrances; Each man in his time plays many parts.
> — WILLIAM SHAKESPEARE

What do I believe about me?

I believe I am smart.

What are my strengths, talents and abilities?

I am good with children.
I am a good team player.
I am a good listener.

How do I express my uniqueness?

I always wear bright colors.

How do I value and reward myself?

Gold stars.

What makes my heart sing?

A beautiful sunrise.
Spring rain
Finishing a job before deadline.

2

tool to focus on the positive aspects of your life — what is good now and what you want to be even better. Answering the questions thoughtfully and positively will give you a clearer picture of your purpose and your passions.

Repeating the affirmations at the bottom of the pages will help to remind your subconscious mind of who you are and who you are becoming.

Realize Who You Are

I am . . .

Strong

Capable

Fun

Wild

Smart

I am becoming . . .

More professional

More knowledgeable about my job

A good communicator

Loving

I Love You!

Affirmation:
My life has endless possibilities. I allow myself the freedom to explore my options. All things are possible with planning, purpose and passion. I am more than enough.

3

Visioning Pages

Get a Clear Picture

There are eight visioning pages in this journal — one for each area of your life. These are the pages on which you will paste the images of the things you desire. To reinforce your images, continue to paste pictures and words throughout your journal. There are no rules as to how it will look when you are finished. You may be surprised when later you turn a page and find that the image you placed there has already materialized. Cut pictures of the things you want to have and the places you want to go from magazines or create them on your computer with clip art and drawing tools. Paste the pictures onto your visioning pages. These pages become the physical expression of your dreams. Be wild and creative. There are no limits to what you can put on your pages. This is a collage of what you want to see in your life. Look at these pages each time you pick up your journal. Imprint them on your mind. Affirm positively, out loud, that you will achieve them.

List the benefits

It is important to identify the benefits you will derive from attaining your goals. Make a list of any way you will benefit from each of your goals either during the process or after attainment. Focus on your rewards. Why should you be motivated? What positive consequences will you enjoy when you put your plan in motion? Visualize the rewards that achieving your goals will bring. Visualize clearly and vividly. Make it such a clear picture that you'll do almost anything to be a part of it. When you drive toward that image, you are motivated.

Affirmations

Affirmations are powerful, positive statements that you would like to believe about yourself. Say or write these in first person tense. These are commands you consciously give to your subconscious mind.

Some examples are:

"All things are possible to me if I believe."
"Every day in every way, my life is getting better and better."
"Everything I need is within me."
"I am smart. I can find a solution."
"I have the courage to do whatever it takes."

The human brain will guide us toward a realization of the mental self image that we have programmed. Your subconscious will work only in the direction you point it. This positive, simple self-talk, when repeated regularly and continuously, will be accepted by the subconscious part of your mind as reality. Repeating your self-talk leads the mind to a state of consciousness where it accepts that which you wish it to believe. The subconscious believes whatever you tell it. In the beginning it may seem to argue with you. You say, "I'm at my perfect weight." And it says, "No, you're not." That's because you've been telling yourself that you are overweight for such a long, long time, your mind has come to believe you are overweight. Now, you must correct your previous misguided instructions and tell your subconcious what you want it to believe. You must repeat your affirmations regularly for a period of no less than twenty-one days in order to override the belief system you now have in place.

You will find affirmations throughout this journal. Choose the ones that resonate with you and repeat frequently until your subconscious accepts them as truth.

Paste your pictures here

Health

Take a Bike Trip in Europe.

Picnic with the family!

I ♥ Exercise

Try the New Fat-Busters!

eat healthy-no more fast foods!

Quit Smoking Now!

I CAN DO IT!

TAKE time to Relax

Organic Facials
Saturday Special
Pretty Woman Spa

New place on Main
Try it!

Go to yoga class and practice poses 15 min per night.

Affirmation:
I honor my body, mind and soul by giving them the nourishment and exercise they need to thrive.

5

The SMART Method of Goal Setting

Writing your goals out, using the SMART method is the first step to making your dreams become reality. SMART goals make it easy to stay on track and resist temptation that may attempt to side-track you. The acronym stands for Specific, Measurable, Agreed upon, Realistic, Time framed.

Specific

Be very specific when writing your goals. Detail every aspect. Writing down your specific goals clarifies exactly where you are going and how you will know when you have arrived. Do not write vague or abstract generalities. Be sure you know exactly what you want to do, be, and have as well as where you want to go. How will it look? What color will it be? How big is it? What will it sound like? How will it smell? What are the details or accessories? How will it feel to have it, do it, be it or go there?

Measurable

Measurement is how we keep track of our progress and how we know if and when we begin to veer off the charted path.

Assess where you are now in relation to where you want to go. By evaluating your current position, you will be able to measure the distance between where you are and your destination. This will enable you to write sub-goals for the steps you will need to take. Also, you can identify changes you may want to make along the way. Take a close look at your current title, income, residence — anything that reaching your goals may change in the future. With a realistic assessment of your current situation, you will be better able to set achievable goals.

Agreed upon

If there are other people whose cooperation you need in order to reach your goal, you need to get their agreement early in the journey. If they don't agree to do their part or to support you in achieving your goals, your journey will be more difficult than need be or it may not be attainable at all.

Realistic

When your goals aren't realistic, you are setting yourself up to fail before you have even started. Your goals must be high enough to motivate you and still be realistic. If you don't believe they are realistic, self-doubt will set in and undermine you causing you to become immobilized. Ask yourself if your goals will create conflict in any other areas of your life. How far are you willing to go to get what you want?

Ascertaining what you want requires self-examination to determine the extent to which your skills, beliefs, values and attitudes relate to your objectives. You will be more likely to succeed if your objectives evolve from your natural abilities and a positive attitude. Achieving your goals requires a high sense of priority that will require belief and discipline. Don't be concerned with how realistic these goals appear to anyone else. Just be sure you believe you can do what you have set out to do.

Time framed

Set a time line and determine checkpoints in order to keep track of your progression toward your goal. Remember, big visions take time to materialize. Identify several smaller goals you must accomplish to reach your big one. As you reach each small goal, reward yourself and move on to the next. It is important to celebrate your successes as you go. Recognizing your achievements along the way will help you to keep a positive attitude throughout the journey.

If you don't have a time designated as to when you will accomplish your goal, you probably won't accomplish it at all. If it doesn't matter when it gets done, it usually doesn't get done. Start your plan with the final objective and work backwards, making sure to allow enough time for each step. Knowing what we intend to accomplish and when we want to accomplish it keeps us focused as well as letting us know if we are ahead or behind our intended schedule.

Make sure you have given yourself realistic time frames. Time lines are set as a means of breaking projects down into smaller, bite-sized chunks so we don't feel overwhelmed. They are not meant to stress us out or make us feel guilty. They are observable criteria that ensure our steady progress rather than leaving it to chance. Good intentions are nice, but a good plan is powerful and a time line is essential to your success.

I will get to my perfect weight by my birthday.

To achieve my perfect weight:

1. I will maintain my daily health regimen by doing fifteen minutes of aerobic exercise three times a week, following my diet five days a week.

Get at least six hours sleep each night within thirty days of starting this journal.

2. Within ninety days of starting this journal, I will increase my exercise to thirty minutes of aerobic exercise three times a week and walk a mile two days a week.

3. I will repeat my health affirmation every morning and every evening.

Journaling

Journaling is a very personal undertaking. Whether you choose to write daily, weekly or whenever the mood strikes you, there are some guidelines to follow that will help you stay on track. Writing your thoughts gives you an opportunity to see what you are thinking. When you can see your thoughts on paper, you can edit and clarify. Having a written history of your thoughts and actions allows you to celebrate how far you've come and plan your next steps.

It is not important how much you write or whether you write daily. It is important that you write as often as possible. Whatever you write should be positive and definite. How you write is an important aspect of successful journaling. Avoid negative words like *not, won't, don't,* or *can't.* . . . The more you program your thinking with positive, definite statements, the easier it is to become that change you are seeking. If you want to record all of your hurts, disappointments and failures, keep a diary. Journaling is a chronicle of your path to who you are and a road map to become who you want to be. This *Achievement Journal* is the record of the steps you are taking to achieve your dreams.

Be sure to give yourself gold stars or stickers for your accomplishments. Rewarding yourself for a job well done feels good. Pictures are as important as words. By adding pictures, stickers, and stars you help reinforce the visualization of your dreams and your successes. You can see at a glance the progress you are making.

Weekly Goals

Personal:

Stay on my diet.

Finish Reading Gone With The Wind

Call Debbie for lunch date

Volunteer at PTA meeting

Professional:

Complete the Stevens project at work

Self-Improvement:

Read You Are More Than Enough

I believe in miracles.

Date 2/13/08

Went out to lunch with the gang at work and stayed on my diet. I even enjoyed the salad. It wasn't easy but I get a gold star for sticking to it. I'm proud of myself.

The Stevens project is on schedule. I want to step up the pace so we can bring it in early. If we can finish before the end of the week, we can bring it in under budget.

My possibilities are endless.

Date 2/14/08

I had a nice chat with Debbie. We're going to do lunch on Friday and catch up. I'm glad I called. I've missed talking with her.

Tonight, the kids are on a sleepover, Jim is at his conference, so I am treating myself to a glass of wine and some quiet time to read my book. Scarlet is chasing Rhett. Can't wait to see what she does next.

Tomorrow, I will make time o read the new inserts for the employee manual.

I am created for success.

Date 2/15/08

I've finished Gone With The Wind. I want to read something that will help me understand how to deal with difficult clients. Even though the Stevens project will be finished today early and under budget, Mr. Stevens is giving everyone in the office a hard time. I want to learn how to hear what his real issue is.

Can't wait to see Debbie tomorrow. It's been a long time.

6

The Balance Wheel

Every twenty-one days, you will find a page with a balance wheel listing the eight areas of your life. In each section of the balance wheel, there are the numbers one to ten. Rate how you are doing in that area of your life on the scale of one to ten. One being poor, ten being excellent. Circle the number. When you have each area scored, connect the dots with a line.

If you have a perfectly round circle or something fairly close to a round circle from a five outward, then you are doing alright at keeping your life in balance.

If you have a perfectly round circle or something close to it from a five or below, you may be in balance, but you need work in all areas of your life.

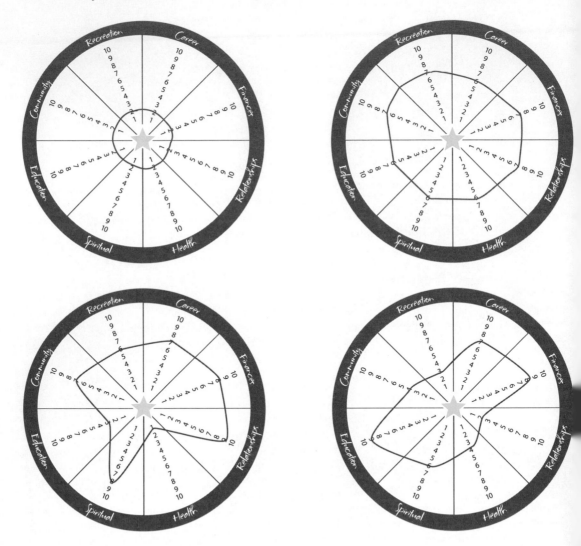

It you have something that looks more like a constellation or an ameba, then you will be abl[e] to see at a glance which area of your life needs a bit more concentration and attention in the nex[t] twenty-one day period.

By evaluating the balance in your life on a regular basis, you should be able to see pending crisis before they happen and avert them.

Balance Wheel

Good for Me!!!

Be aware of wonder. Live a balanced life — learn some and think some and draw and paint and sing and dance and play and work every day some.
—ROBERT FULGHUM

Milestones

Following each balance wheel page is a place to record milestones. It is important to recognize our progress. Wherever you are along the path toward your ultimate goal, you have done good things. Even if it is only a small step, it is progress. Acknowledge yourself for what you have already accomplished, and then determine the next steps to take from there. As you assess your progress, re-evaluate your goals and time frames.

Milestones

I feel good about what I have accomplished so far.

I stayed on my diet and ate healthy food every day.

I've lost 6 pounds!!!!!!

The Stevens project came in early and under budget because of my planning and determination.

I finished *Gone With the Wind* and two other books.

The next step toward my goal is easy.

Organize my desk at work so it is easy to work.

Find a seminar or someone to mentor me in dealing with difficult people.

Spend more time with Jim so he knows how much I appreciate him.

9

This is the beginning
of a life filled with
Purpose, Passion & Power

This is the beginning
of a life filled with
Purpose, Passion & Power

My Greatest Achievements So Far

We all have milestones in our lives. These are the events that stand out as turning points and mark the passage of time. From the gold star in kindergarten for good manners to our most recent promotion, these are the successes that have defined who we are. List yours below:

_____

_____

_____

_____

_____

_____

_____

_____

_____

_____

_____

_____

_____

_____

_____

_____

_____

_____

_____

_____

_____

_____

Affirmation:
My life is a journey of becoming the person I was meant to be. I am more than enough!

Realize Who You Are

What do I believe about me?

_____

_____

_____

_____

What are my strengths, talents and abilities?

_____

_____

_____

_____

How do I express my uniqueness?

_____

_____

_____

_____

How do I value and reward myself?

_____

_____

_____

_____

What makes my heart sing?

_____

_____

_____

_____

I am . . .

_____

_____

_____

_____

_____

_____

_____

_____

_____

_____

I am becoming . . .

_____

_____

_____

_____

_____

_____

_____

_____

_____

_____

Affirmation:

All that I am, all that I will be is within me now. I recognize who I am now and who I am destined to become. I allow my innermost self to show me the wonder of how my life can be. I am more than enough.

Explore Your Possibilities

What would I love to do, have and be?

What can I do to make it possible?

Where will I start?

Who can help me make this a reality?

What is the absolute worst possible thing that can happen if I try? Can I live with that?

My wishes . . .

My dreams . . .

My opportunities . . .

Affirmation:

My life has endless possibilities. I allow myself the freedom to explore my options. All things are possible with planning, purpose and passion. I am more than enough.

Choose Your Future

What do I do well?

What am I passionate about?

What are my values and priorities?

When do I feel most needed and appreciated?

Which of my talents, skills and abilities am I using now?

In a year . . .

_____

_____

_____

In five years . . .

_____

_____

_____

In ten years . . .

_____

_____

_____

When I am old . . .

_____

_____

_____

My tombstone . . .

_____

_____

_____

My legacy . . .

_____

_____

_____

Affirmation:

I know what I want. I have a clear picture of how I want to be and what I want to do.
I work toward the achievement of my goals everyday. I achieve my desires through the
knowledge of my purpose, the passion of my desire and the power of my commitment.
I am more than enough.

Imagine You Are There

What do I want to become?

_____

_____

_____

_____

What do I daydream about?

_____

_____

_____

_____

What would I do if I had the courage to go after my dreams?

_____

_____

_____

_____

Where will I begin?

_____

_____

_____

_____

What does my future hold?

_____

_____

_____

_____

This is a portrait of my dreams, my goals, my life. . . .

Paste your pictures here.

Affirmation:

I can see the picture of where I'm going and the road I'm taking to get there. I paint my own picture of how it will be. My life is my masterpiece. I am more than enough.

Talk Yourself Into It

To establish true self-esteem, we must concentrate on our successes and forget about the failures and negatives in our lives.
— Denis Waitley

What do I say when I talk to myself?

_____

_____

_____

_____

What do I say when things don't go as I think they should?

_____

_____

_____

_____

What can I say that would be more positive?

_____

_____

_____

_____

What do I say when someone asks how I am? What did I mean?

_____

_____

_____

_____

What would I like to believe about me?

_____

_____

_____

_____

PSST . . . my personal affirmations:

Affirmation:

I give myself the love and support I need. I speak to myself with encouragement, acceptance and kindness. My words have the power to heal and nurture my self image. I allow myself to believe the truth of the beauty that lies within me. As I speak, so I become. I am more than enough.

Believe You Can

What excites me?

What do I love?

What do I secretly wish I could do?

What would I do even if I didn't get paid?

What are my special talents?

I believe I can . . .

_____

_____

_____

_____

_____

_____

_____

_____

_____

_____

_____

_____

_____

_____

_____

_____

_____

_____

_____

_____

_____

_____

_____

_____

Affirmation:

No matter how high, no matter how far, I set my sights upon my star. I can reach it because I believe I can. I believe in me. I believe in my dreams. I believe in my worth. I believe in my power to become the best me I can be. I am more than enough.

Make Life Work For You

People are always blaming their circumstances for what they are. I don't believe in circumstances. The people who get on in this world are the people who get up and look for the circumstances they want, and if they can't find them, make them.

— George Bernard Shaw

What do I love about my life?

What steps am I taking to accomplish my goals?

What can I do differently?

What and to whom can I delegate?

How am I using my time to efficiently and effectively accomplish my goals?

My personal contract with myself . . .

I _____,

do hereby declare and affirm that I am committed to my success. Now, therefore, I

pledge to the following:

_____

_____

_____

_____

_____

_____

_____

_____

_____

_____

_____ Date_____

Signature_____

Affirmation:

I accept responsibility for how my life works. I get off the bench and into the game.
I make things happen that will bring the success and joy I dream of into my life.
I am more than enough.

Say What You Mean

The problem with communication . . . is the illusion that it has been accomplished.
— George Bernard Shaw

Am I getting the results I want? If not, why not?

Which of my behaviors do I need to change?

Do I modulate my voice to show respect to others — even in disagreement?

Am I asking the right questions?

Do I listen for understanding?

To communicate more clearly, I will:

_____
_____
_____
_____
_____
_____
_____
_____

Who do I need to listen to?

_____
_____
_____
_____
_____
_____
_____
_____
_____

What do I want to communicate about myself?

_____
_____
_____
_____
_____
_____
_____
_____

Affirmation:

I am confident and secure. It is safe for me to speak the truth about what I want. I can say "no" when that is what I mean. I get what I want because I am clear in my communication with myself and others. I am more than enough.

Establish Your Look

Create your own visual style . . . let it be unique
for yourself and yet identifiable for others.
— ORSON WELLES

What message does my appearance communicate to others?

What am I attempting to achieve with my appearance?

What does my posture and body language say about me?

What impressions do others form about me based on my facial expressions and demeanor?

What do I need to do to project a sense of authority, presence and trust?

How I see myself:

_____

_____

_____

_____

_____

_____

_____

_____

_____

Changes I must make to bring my appearance into alignment with my vision:

_____

_____

_____

_____

_____

_____

_____

_____

_____

_____

_____

Affirmation:

My outward appearance is in perfect harmony with who I am becoming. People see me as strong, trustworthy, knowledgeable and successful. I make a memorable impression wherever I go. I look the part I am living. I am more than enough.

Associate for Success

Who are my friends and associates?

What do I need to learn from these people?

How do they support the pursuit of my goals?

What groups or organizations would be the most beneficial to my growth?

What do I need to do to build a powerful network?

Who are my heroes and role models?

Who are my mentors?

Who could benefit from my knowledge and experience?

Affirmation:

I put myself in the right place at the right time. I cultivate the friendships and associations that support my success. My attitude and demeanor attract people who want to help me reach my goals. My willingness to share and help others opens the door to even greater circles of success. I am more than enough.

Overcoming Life's Obstacles

Difficulties meet us at every turn. They are the accompaniment of life. Out of pain grow the violets of patience and sweetness. The richness of the human experience would lose something of rewarding joy if there were no limitations to overcome.
—Helen Keller

What obstacles do I foresee?

What talents, skills and knowledge do I need and how can I get them?

Who do I need to ask for help?

What old hurts, beliefs and experiences do I need to let go of?

What changes do I need to make?

My Stumbling Blocks . . .

My Stepping Stones . . .

Affirmation:

I am smart, creative, and resourceful. I look for opportunities instead of obstacles.
I use my skills and talents to move mountains and build bridges wherever necessary.
I handle adversity with poise, grace, and power and move steadfastly toward my dreams.
I am more than enough.

Achieve Power Through Faith

Is a diamond less valuable because it is covered with mud?
God sees the changeless beauty of our souls. He knows we are not our mistakes.
— PARAMAHANSA YOGANANDA

What do I believe?

How do I balance my physical, mental and spiritual life?

How do I express or live my beliefs?

How do I honor myself, my family, my community and my beliefs?

Who and what am I thankful for?

Steps I will take to strengthen my faith:

Steps I will take to demonstrate my faith:

Affirmation:

*I believe in the power within me to become the person I was meant to be. I align myself
and my desires with the abundance of good that is waiting for me to claim it. I am
centered and anchored in my faith. I am more than enough.*

With Gratitude . . .

Cheerleaders, mentors, listeners and friends:

Affirmation:

My friends and family support my dreams. I can call on them to cheer my successes and remind me of my goals when I lose my way. I am more than enough.

Ways to Make Life Work

I find the great thing in this world is not so much where we stand as in what direction we are moving.
—OLIVER WENDELL HOLMES

Give up blame

Blame shifts the responsibility of our lives and our happiness, making it someone else's responsibility. Your life is your responsibility and only yours.

Stop making excuses

Making excuses is another way we shift responsibility. Instead of blaming people, we blame things or circumstances. Remember, where there is a will there is a way.

Learn to live in the present

Instead of being passive, do something about your dream. The present is the only time we have. Start by doing the best you can whatever you are doing.

Become a problem solver

Problem identifiers are a dime a dozen. Anyone can go around pointing out problems. On the other hand, problem solvers are worth their weight in gold.

Make every moment count

Today we do everything fast: talk fast, drive fast, even eat fast. Time is at a premium and most of us are afflicted with *hurry sickness*.

Set your priorities

Decide right now that you are going to start making every moment of your life count by doing what is important to you with those who are most important in your life. Do the most important things first.

Make decisions quickly

Once you have all the available facts, make a decision. Rarely does delay improve the quality of choice.

Delegate regularly

Whether in a corporate environment, or at home, delegate to others. If done right, delegation is a learning experience and a motivator.

Control interruptions, time wasters, and distractions

Interruptions and distractions can be treacherous. Look for patterns in interruptions.

Take action

Action is our only choice. Without it, we become stagnant, like a ship at anchor, we'll go nowhere. If we are to reach our destination, we must take specific and direct action.

Affirmation:
My life works. I have the time, energy, and skills I need to succeed.
I am more than enough.

Specific

Measurable

Agreed Upon

Realistic

Time Framed

Career

Write your career goals here. Remember to be SMART!

Paste your pictures here.

Affirmation:
I love what I do and I do it with love.

Financial

Write your financial goals here. Remember to be SMART!

Paste your pictures here.

Affirmation:
I am richly rewarded for all that I do.

Relationships

Write your relationship goals here. Remember to be SMART!

Paste your pictures here.

Affirmation:
My relationships are healthy, loving and fulfilling.

Health

Write your health goals here. Remember to be SMART!

Paste your pictures here.

Affirmation:
I honor my body, mind and soul by giving them the nourishment and exercise they need to thrive.

Spiritual

Write your spiritual goals here. Remember to be SMART!

Paste your pictures here.

Affirmation:
I am centered in the truth of who I am.

Educational

Write your educational goals here. Remember to be SMART!

Paste your pictures here.

Affirmation:

I learn something new about my life, my family, my friends or my world every day.

Community

Write your goals for supporting your community here. Remember to be SMART!

Paste your pictures here.

Affirmation:
I give back to my community to bring new light to the world.

Recreation

Write your rest and relaxation goals here. Remember to be SMART!

Paste your pictures here.

Affirmation:
*I give myself the gift of
time to play and relax.*

If I knew I could not fail . . .

I would . . .

Affirmation:

I am free of barriers to my success. I can do whatever my heart desires. I find my purpose, pursue it with passion, and enjoy the powerful fulfillment of my dreams.

Listen to the Exhortation of the Dawn!

Look to this Day!

For it is Life, the very Life of Life.

In its brief course lie all the

Verities and Realities of your Existence.

The Bliss of Growth,

The Glory of Action,

The Splendor of Beauty;

For Yesterday is but a Dream,

And Tomorrow is only a Vision;

But Today well lived makes

Every Yesterday a Dream of Happiness,

And every Tomorrow a Vision of Hope.

Look well therefore to this Day!

Such is the Salutation of the Dawn!

— Kalidasa

Weekly Goals

_____   _____
_____   _____
_____   _____
_____   _____
_____   _____
_____   _____

I am created for success.   Date
_____
_____
_____
_____

My possibilities are endless.   Date
_____
_____
_____
_____

My potential is unlimited.   Date
_____
_____
_____
_____
_____

I am powerful, calm and centered.   Date

_____

_____

_____

_____

_____

Health, happiness and prosperity are mine.   Date

_____

_____

_____

_____

_____

I am free of fear.   Date

_____

_____

_____

_____

_____

I have faith and confidence.   Date

_____

_____

_____

_____

_____

Weekly Goals

_____   _____
_____   _____
_____   _____
_____   _____
_____   _____
_____   _____
_____

There is great genius within me.   Date
_____
_____
_____
_____

I have fun daily.   Date
_____
_____
_____
_____

I live with purpose and passion.   Date
_____
_____
_____
_____

I am living a values based life.   Date

I am crystal clear about my life purpose.   Date

I am making things happen.   Date

I show appreciation to others.   Date

Weekly Goals

_____   _____
_____   _____
_____   _____
_____   _____
_____   _____
_____   _____

My story has just begun.   Date

_____
_____
_____
_____

I eat responsibly and take care of my body.   Date

_____
_____
_____
_____

My life is free of unnecessary clutter.   Date

_____
_____
_____
_____
_____

I take responsibility for my thoughts, my actions and my life.   Date

_____

_____

_____

_____

_____

I love and accept myself.   Date

_____

_____

_____

_____

_____

I pay attention to details.   Date

_____

_____

_____

_____

_____

Miracles are happening for me now.   Date

_____

_____

_____

_____

_____

Balance Wheel

*Be aware of wonder. Live a balanced life — learn
some and think some and draw and paint and sing
and dance and play and work every day some.*
—ROBERT FULGHUM

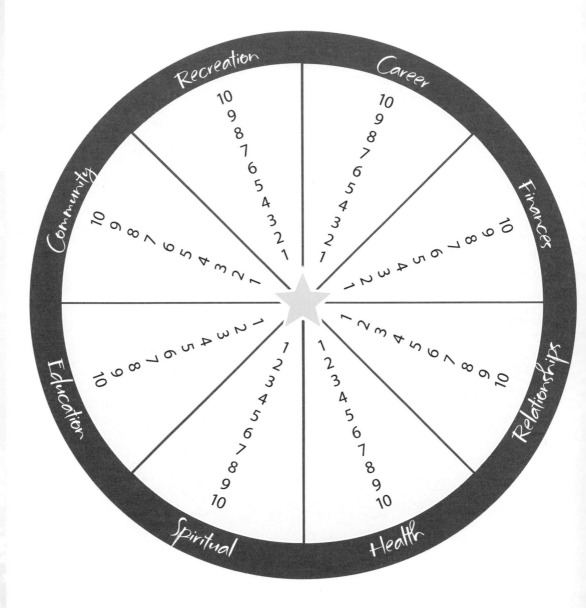

I feel good about what I have accomplished so far.

The next step toward my goal is easy.

Weekly Goals

_____   _____
_____   _____
_____   _____
_____   _____
_____   _____
_____   _____

I am a creative person.   Date
_____
_____
_____
_____
_____

I have many choices.   Date
_____
_____
_____
_____
_____

My life is joyous.   Date
_____
_____
_____
_____
_____

Beautiful, bright ideas come to me naturally.   Date

I am in my perfect place.   Date

I use my time wisely.   Date

I recognize the miracles that happen every day.   Date

Weekly Goals

_____   _____
_____   _____
_____   _____
_____   _____
_____   _____
_____   _____
_____   _____

The best of everything is mine.   Date

_____
_____
_____
_____

I am strong and confident.   Date

_____
_____
_____
_____

My dreams are coming true.   Date

_____
_____
_____
_____
_____

I am free of doubt and fear.   Date

Prosperity is flowing into my life right now.   Date

Passion is the fuel that powers my desires.   Date

I acknowledge the greatness within me.   Date

Weekly Goals

_____   _____
_____   _____
_____   _____
_____   _____
_____   _____
_____   _____

My self-confidence helps my relationships thrive.   Date

_____
_____
_____
_____
_____

Life is exciting and I live with enthusiasm.   Date

_____
_____
_____
_____
_____

I'm well prepared to handle my life situations.   Date

_____
_____
_____
_____
_____

My past has no power over me now.   Date

I unleash my passion for life and fulfill my dreams.   Date

I nurture my creativity daily.   Date

I listen to my inner voice.   Date

Balance Wheel

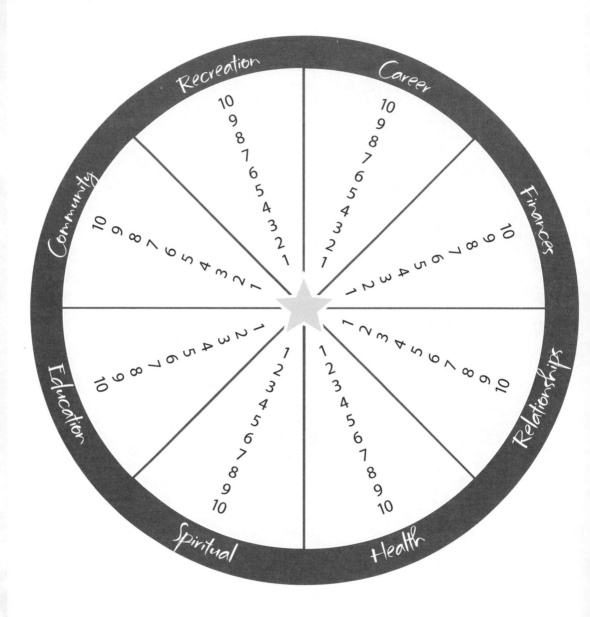

I feel good about what I have accomplished so far.

The next step toward my goal is easy.

Weekly Goals

_____   _____

_____   _____

_____   _____

_____   _____

_____   _____

_____   _____

_____

I am destined to do great things. _____ Date _____

_____

_____

_____

_____

_____

The only person who can change my life is me. _____ Date _____

_____

_____

_____

_____

_____

I am peaceful, calm and centered. _____ Date _____

_____

_____

_____

_____

_____

I create a positive lasting impression everywhere I go.   Date

Every day brings me closer to the fulfillment of my dreams.   Date

I accept complete responsibility for my life.   Date

I honor my body, my mind and my spirit.   Date

Weekly Goals

_____   _____
_____   _____
_____   _____
_____   _____
_____   _____
_____   _____

I am always in the right place at the right time.   Date

_____
_____
_____
_____
_____

There are lots of good times to come.   Date

_____
_____
_____
_____
_____

I enjoy a positive personal relationship.   Date

_____
_____
_____
_____
_____

I have the tools and talents to succeed.   Date

I know where I'm going and how to get there.   Date

I accept my prosperity graciously.   Date

I live today with excitement, expectation and wonder.   Date

Weekly Goals

_____   _____
_____   _____
_____   _____
_____   _____
_____   _____
_____   _____

My purpose is clear, my passion is strong, my power is great.   Date

I always have more than I need.   Date

I am a unique individual.   Date

I choose the roles I will play in life.   Date

I am attracting loving relationships into my life.   Date

With enthusiasm, purpose, and passion, I feel the power   Date

surge forth to manifest my desires.

I experience the essence of power as peace, calm and confidence.   Date

Balance Wheel

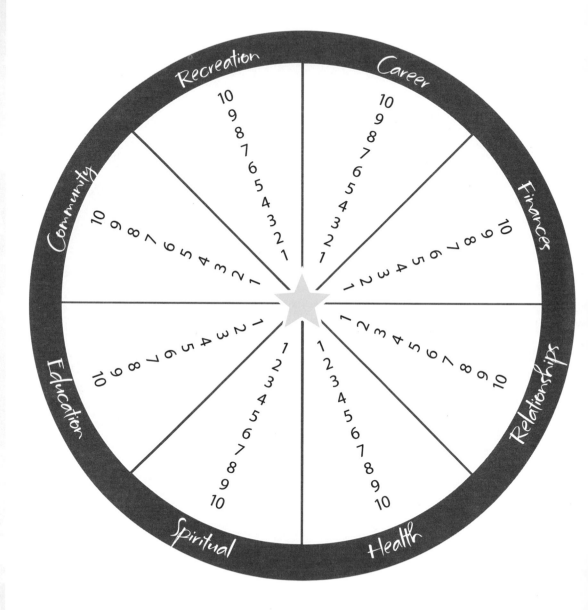

I feel good about what I have accomplished so far.

The next step toward my goal is easy.

Weekly Goals

_____   _____

_____   _____

_____   _____

_____   _____

_____   _____

_____   _____

I move beyond my perceived limitations.   Date

_____

_____

_____

_____

I am loving and kind.   Date

_____

_____

_____

_____

I am understanding of people different than me.   Date

_____

_____

_____

_____

I live in the present moment and have a positive outlook.   Date

I hone my talents and use them to succeed.   Date

I am big enough, strong enough and smart enough to do   Date
whatever I want to do.

I bless my financial situation and know abundance is mine.   Date

Weekly Goals

_____   _____

_____   _____

_____   _____

_____   _____

_____   _____

_____   _____

I have the power to change my life.   Date

_____

_____

_____

_____

I improve my skills everyday.   Date

_____

_____

_____

_____

I am experiencing quality in living.   Date

_____

_____

_____

_____

I am consciously aware of my thoughts.   Date

I am determined and disciplined to achieve my goals.   Date

I constantly strive to be 1% better than yesterday.   Date

I give thanks for my success.   Date

Weekly Goals

_____   _____

_____   _____

_____   _____

_____   _____

_____   _____

_____   _____

_____   _____

My resources are inexhaustible.   Date
_____

_____

_____

_____

_____

My purpose is clear to me now.   Date
_____

_____

_____

_____

_____

My heart soars with joy with every success.   Date
_____

_____

_____

_____

_____

My life is filled with great experiences.   Date

I am awake to all the possibilities before me.   Date

I choose energy, enthusiasm and excitement.   Date

I believe in myself and the power of my dreams.   Date

Balance Wheel

Be aware of wonder. Live a balanced life — learn some and think some and draw and paint and sing and dance and play and work every day some.
—ROBERT FULGHUM

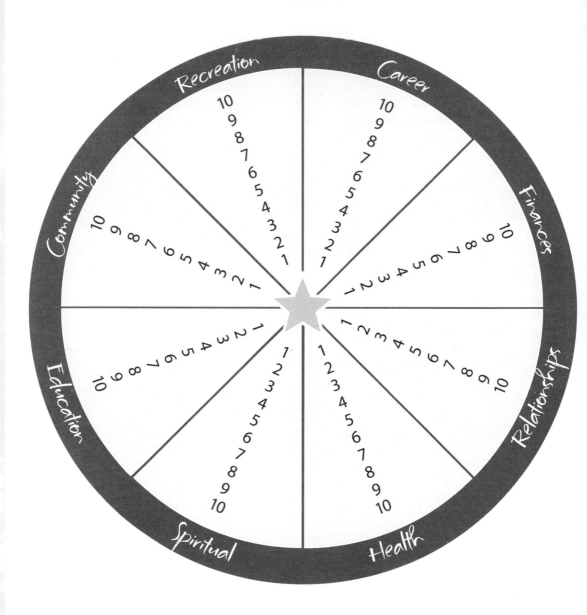

I feel good about what I have accomplished so far.

The next step toward my goal is easy.

Weekly Goals

_____   _____
_____   _____
_____   _____
_____   _____
_____   _____
_____   _____
_____   _____

I make choices that are right for me and those around me.   Date
_____
_____
_____
_____
_____

I am committed to a purposeful, passionate life.   Date
_____
_____
_____
_____
_____

I like the way I feel when I am living on purpose.   Date
_____
_____
_____
_____
_____
_____

I am committed to my goals.   Date

I am excited about my purpose.   Date

I enjoy the freedom of an unlimited life.   Date

I am in harmony with myself and my world.   Date

Weekly Goals

_____   _____
_____   _____
_____   _____
_____   _____
_____   _____
_____

I live a life of happiness and joy.   Date
_____
_____
_____
_____

I give because I choose to give, not because I should.   Date
_____
_____
_____
_____

I am free of pretense because I am all that I feel I should be.   Date
_____
_____
_____
_____

I can and do make a difference in the world.   Date

I focus on positive, successful traits in myself and others.   Date

I find joy in my ability to overcome adversity.   Date

I give up struggle, suffering and stress and accept peace,   Date
purpose and passion.

Weekly Goals

_____   _____

_____   _____

_____   _____

_____   _____

_____   _____

_____   _____

_____

I give my best every day. _____   Date _____

_____

_____

_____

_____

I am creating the life I desire. _____   Date _____

_____

_____

_____

_____

I live on purpose. _____   Date _____

_____

_____

_____

_____

_____

I find something good in every situation.   Date

I have enough time, love, and energy to do whatever needs   Date
to be done.

I am aware of the power of my words.   Date

I find peace in living with purpose, passion and power.   Date

Balance Wheel

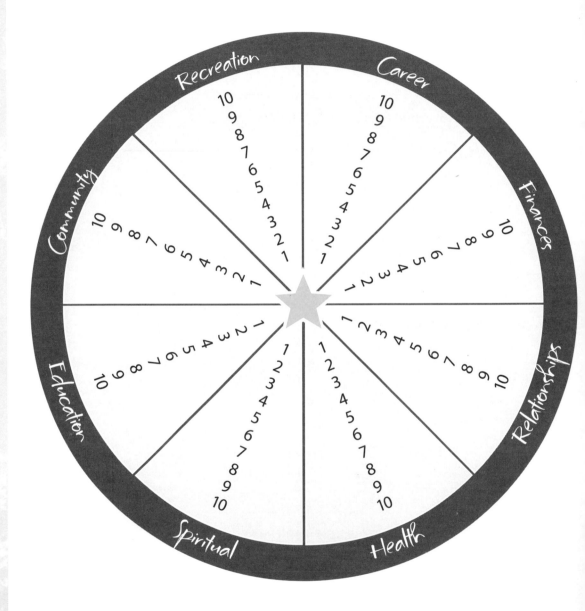

I feel good about what I have accomplished so far.

The next step toward my goal is easy.

Weekly Goals

_____   _____
_____   _____
_____   _____
_____   _____
_____   _____
_____   _____

I have confidence in my knowledge and talent.   Date

_____
_____
_____
_____
_____

I claim my freedom and success.   Date

_____
_____
_____
_____
_____

I am filled with energy and enthusiasm.   Date

_____
_____
_____
_____
_____

I am grateful for the joys in my life.   Date

I attract positive, loving, supportive and enthusiastic people   Date

into my life.

I live purposefully, passionately and with great enthusiasm.   Date

I am grateful for the miracle of change.   Date

Weekly Goals

_____   _____
_____   _____
_____   _____
_____   _____
_____   _____
_____   _____

I listen to what my body wants and needs.   Date

_____
_____
_____
_____

My relationships are healthy and empowering.   Date

_____
_____
_____
_____

I am free to be the me I choose to be.   Date

_____
_____
_____
_____

I am intelligent, capable and worthy.   Date

I approach problems in a calm and relaxed manner.   Date

I ask lots of questions so that I can know the truth.   Date

I experience the peace and wonder of a life lived on purpose.   Date

Weekly Goals

_____   _____

_____   _____

_____   _____

_____   _____

_____   _____

_____   _____

I have the ability to achieve my goals.   Date

_____

_____

_____

_____

I attract success.   Date

_____

_____

_____

_____

I feel the joy of sun on my face and wind in my hair   Date

as I swing on the playground of life.

_____

_____

_____

_____

My life is in balance.   Date

I am richly rewarded for my contribution to life.   Date

I am passionate about my dreams.   Date

I listen to the song of my heart.   Date

Balance Wheel

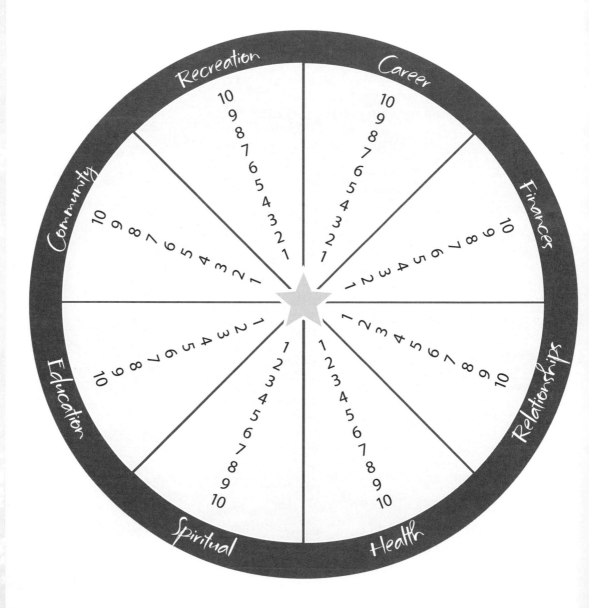

I feel good about what I have accomplished so far.

The next step toward my goal is easy.

Weekly Goals

_____   _____

_____   _____

_____   _____

_____   _____

_____   _____

_____   _____

I bring joy to my family.   Date

_____

_____

_____

_____

I walk the path of peace toward the fulfillment of my desires.   Date

_____

_____

_____

_____

I climb to new heights as I work smarter, not harder.   Date

_____

_____

_____

_____

_____

I take risks to achieve my goals.   Date

I am surrounded by loving, supportive family and friends.   Date

I am responsible for my own well being.   Date

I am filled with gratitude for my blessings   Date

Weekly Goals

_____   _____

_____   _____

_____   _____

_____   _____

_____   _____

_____   _____

I am sophisticated, elegant, and relaxed.   Date

_____

_____

_____

_____

I uncover, recover and discover all that I am and all that I can be.   Date

_____

_____

_____

_____

I believe in the power of my dreams.   Date

_____

_____

_____

_____

_____

I am ready and willing to accept my success.   Date

I approve of myself and my actions.   Date

I expect the best and it comes to me.   Date

I am guided into the right experiences.   Date

Weekly Goals

_____   _____

_____   _____

_____   _____

_____   _____

_____   _____

_____   _____

I eat smart to stay healthy.   Date

_____

_____

_____

_____

_____

I choose my thoughts carefully.   Date

_____

_____

_____

_____

_____

I attract good luck.   Date

_____

_____

_____

_____

_____

I am vibrantly alive and involved.   Date

I am at my perfect weight.   Date

I communicate my desires clearly.   Date

I am open to the vast wonders of life.   Date

Balance Wheel

Be aware of wonder. Live a balanced life — learn some and think some and draw and paint and sing and dance and play and work every day some.
—Robert Fulghum

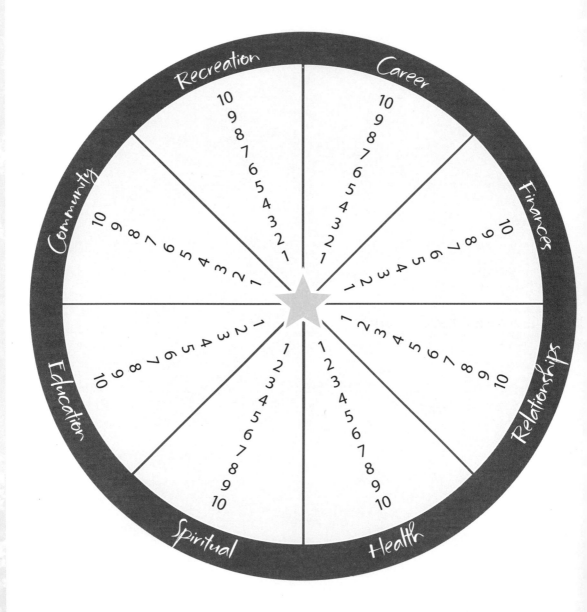

I feel good about what I have accomplished so far.

The next step toward my goal is easy.

Weekly Goals

_____   _____
_____   _____
_____   _____
_____   _____
_____   _____
_____   _____

The resources I need are within my reach.   Date

_____
_____
_____
_____

I give up judgment, criticism, comparison and accept   Date
myself as I am.

_____
_____
_____
_____

I forgive myself.   Date

_____
_____
_____
_____
_____

I choose to be happy.   Date

I handle difficult situations with grace and confidence.   Date

I have faith in my ability to achieve my wildest dreams.   Date

I am surrounded and protected by love.   Date

Weekly Goals

_____   _____
_____   _____
_____   _____
_____   _____
_____   _____
_____   _____

I exercise my body and my mind.   Date

I enjoy loving relationships.   Date

I am safe and secure.   Date

I am responsible for who I am.   Date

I have found my purpose and my peace.   Date

I give up self limiting beliefs.   Date

I live with joy, passion and energy.   Date

Weekly Goals

_____   _____

_____   _____

_____   _____

_____   _____

_____   _____

_____   _____

I am the most important person in my world.   Date

_____

_____

_____

_____

_____

I free myself of barriers in my mind.   Date

_____

_____

_____

_____

_____

I get results.   Date

_____

_____

_____

_____

_____

_____

I give thanks for each new opportunity.   Date

I am worthy of love.   Date

I am the perfect person for the job.   Date

I am receiving abundance right now.   Date

Balance Wheel

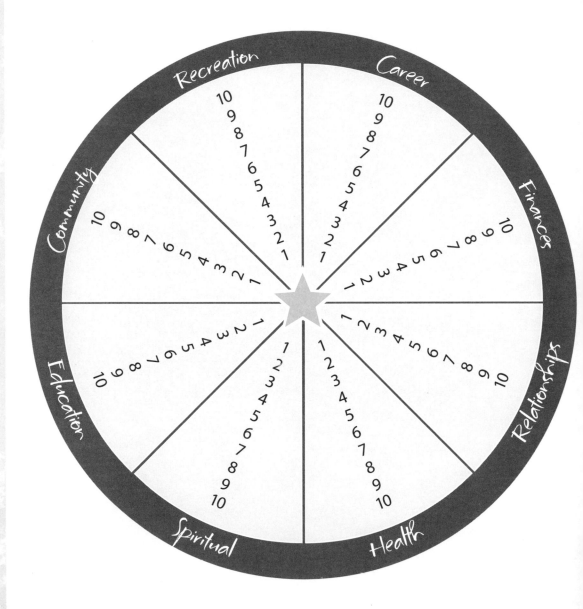

I feel good about what I have accomplished so far.

The next step toward my goal is easy.

_____ _____
_____ _____
_____ _____
_____ _____
_____ _____
_____ _____
_____ _____

I feel compassion for others.   Date
_____
_____
_____
_____
_____

I am the first and only me.   Date
_____
_____
_____
_____
_____

I choose life, love and liberty.   Date
_____
_____
_____
_____
_____

Today I share my joy.   Date

I find joy in simple things.   Date

I have the power to create good in my life.   Date

I exercise my faith and my beliefs.   Date

Weekly Goals

_____   _____
_____   _____
_____   _____
_____   _____
_____   _____
_____

I give up fear and doubt.   Date

I have a serene, elegant feeling in my home.   Date

I love what I do and I do it with love.   Date

I have the power to choose my destiny.   Date

I am open and receptive to receiving my good.   Date

I am the change I have been seeking.   Date

I know how to say "NO" and say it when appropriate.   Date

Weekly Goals

_____   _____

_____   _____

_____   _____

_____   _____

_____   _____

_____   _____

I count my blessings daily.   Date

_____

_____

_____

_____

_____

I hear the song of life in the sounds of nature.   Date

_____

_____

_____

_____

_____

I have a winning attitude.   Date

_____

_____

_____

_____

_____

I let go of fear and leap confidently into the future.   Date

I live each moment fully, with purpose and passion.   Date

I make a difference in the world.   Date

I live in perfect harmony with my family and friends.   Date

Balance Wheel

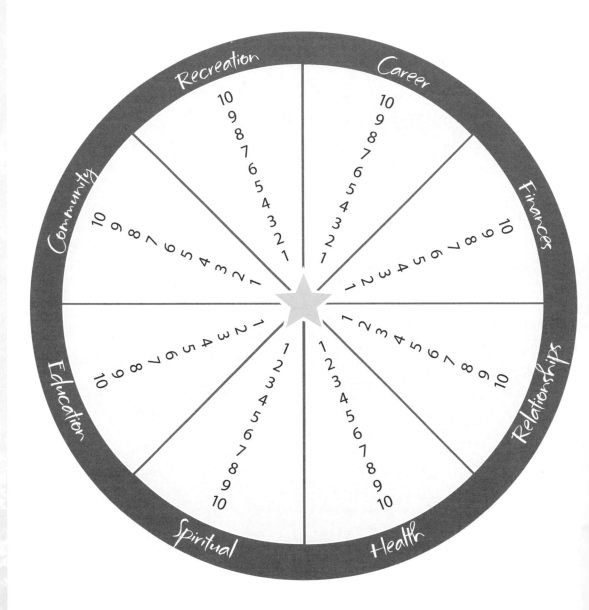

I feel good about what I have accomplished so far.

The next step toward my goal is easy.

Weekly Goals

_____   _____
_____   _____
_____   _____
_____   _____
_____   _____
_____   _____

I am surrounded by beauty and filled with peace.   Date

I hold the keys to my dreams.   Date

I learn something new every day.   Date

I give up my anger.   Date

My positive attitude enhances my experiences.   Date

Knowing my purpose gives me great power.   Date

I listen carefully to my inner voice.   Date

Weekly Goals

_____   _____
_____   _____
_____   _____
_____   _____
_____   _____
_____   _____

I am thankful for my gift of abundance.   Date _____

I let people be who they are.   Date _____

There is always enough time for me.   Date _____

My life is rich and rewarding.   Date

I set positive goals and take action to achieve them.   Date

I stride purposefully in the direction of my dreams.   Date

I am becoming the person I was meant to be.   Date

Weekly Goals

_____   _____
_____   _____
_____   _____
_____   _____
_____   _____
_____   _____
_____   _____

I believe in the power of love.   Date

I believe in me.   Date

I nurture and support myself.   Date

Doors open for my dreams and goals.   Date

I greet others with love.   Date

I have the time and patience to achieve my goals.   Date

I am beautiful, passionate and powerful.   Date

Balance Wheel

Be aware of wonder. Live a balanced life — learn some and think some and draw and paint and sing and dance and play and work every day some.
—Robert Fulghum

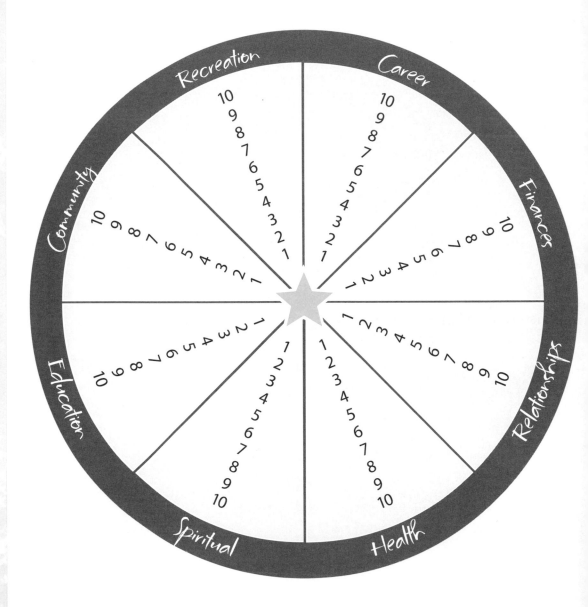

I feel good about what I have accomplished so far.

The next step toward my goal is easy.

Weekly Goals

_____   _____
_____   _____
_____   _____
_____   _____
_____   _____
_____   _____

I take time to renew my energy.   Date

Life brings me positive experiences.   Date

I make sound and wise decisions.   Date

I am filled with the satisfaction of a purposeful life.   Date

I am grateful for this moment.   Date

I have energy to spare.   Date

I am generously rewarded for what I do.   Date

Weekly Goals

_____   _____
_____   _____
_____   _____
_____   _____
_____   _____

My inner strength carries me through any difficulties.   Date

I enjoy peace of mind.   Date

I guard my thoughts and words.   Date

I let go of my past and reach confidently for my future.   Date

I stay off the path to perfection and realize that excellence is   Date
good enough.

I have the power to change my feelings.   Date

I express my gratitude for my wonderful life.   Date

Weekly Goals

_____   _____
_____   _____
_____   _____
_____   _____
_____   _____
_____   _____

I think, feel, speak and act in faith.   Date

I like people and they like me.   Date

I handle conflict with ease.   Date

I let go of things I no longer need.   Date

I look for opportunities to learn new things.   Date

I practice the things that make me successful.   Date

I maintain a positive attitude.   Date

Balance Wheel

Be aware of wonder. Live a balanced life — learn some and think some and draw and paint and sing and dance and play and work every day some.
—ROBERT FULGHUM

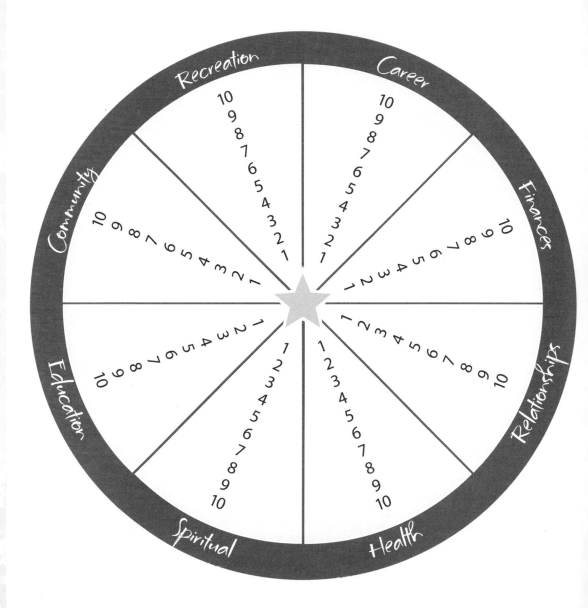

I feel good about what I have accomplished so far.

The next step toward my goal is easy.

Weekly Goals

_____   _____

_____   _____

_____   _____

_____   _____

_____   _____

_____   _____

_____

I am in harmony with life.   Date _____

_____

_____

_____

_____

_____

I recognize opportunities when they knock.   Date _____

_____

_____

_____

_____

_____

I radiate poise, confidence, wisdom and joy.   Date _____

_____

_____

_____

_____

_____

I see the sun, even when it is behind the clouds.   Date

Good things are happening in every area of my life.   Date

I am innovative and creative.   Date

I have the power to make things happen.   Date

Weekly Goals

_____   _____

_____   _____

_____   _____

_____   _____

_____   _____

_____   _____

I am filled with love.   Date

_____

_____

_____

_____

_____

I help those in need.   Date

_____

_____

_____

_____

_____

I laugh often and with joy.   Date

_____

_____

_____

_____

_____

I am filled with strength, courage and peace.   Date

I learn from my mistakes.   Date

I know my purpose.   Date

I live with enthusiasm.   Date

Weekly Goals

_____   _____
_____   _____
_____   _____
_____   _____
_____   _____
_____   _____

I love myself just as I am.   Date

I look forward to the future with joy.   Date

I keep my thoughts positive.   Date

I am the author of my own story. Date

I look good and I feel good. Date

I read books and articles that enrich my life. Date

I live my life with passion. Date

Balance Wheel

*Be aware of wonder. Live a balanced life — learn
some and think some and draw and paint and sing
and dance and play and work every day some.*
—Robert Fulghum

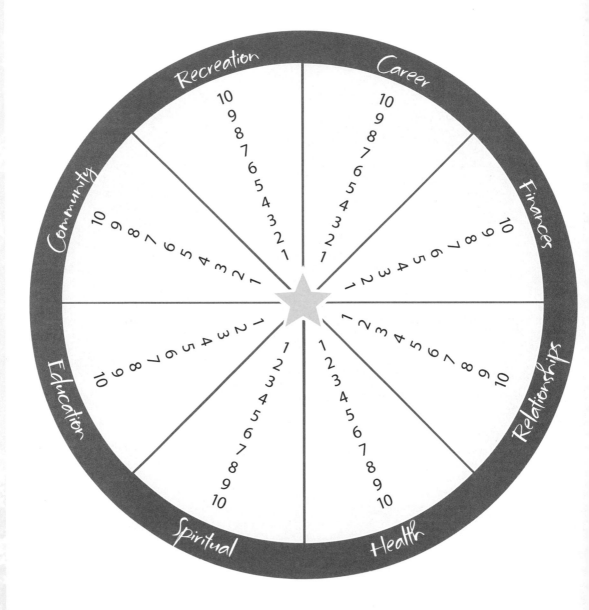

160

I feel good about what I have accomplished so far.

The next step toward my goal is easy.

Weekly Goals

_____

I live in peace and joy.   Date

_____

I love and respect myself.   Date

_____

I take time to rest and reflect.   Date

I am gifted with an unlimited source of supply. Date

Giving back is an expression of gratitude for my own gifts. Date

I get what I want from life. Date

I am unlimited in my abilities. Date

Weekly Goals

_____   _____
_____   _____
_____   _____
_____   _____
_____   _____
_____   _____

Peace and joy surround me.   Date

_____
_____
_____
_____

I show respect for myself.   Date

_____
_____
_____
_____

I love to exercise.   Date

_____
_____
_____
_____
_____

I am on a grand adventure.   Date

I pursue my dreams with passion.   Date

I make decisions with comfort and ease.   Date

I listen carefully to others.   Date

Weekly Goals

_____   _____
_____   _____
_____   _____
_____   _____
_____   _____
_____   _____

I make the right choices.   Date _____

_____
_____
_____
_____
_____

I look on the bright side.   Date _____

_____
_____
_____
_____
_____

I recognize opportunity in the obstacles that present themselves.   Date _____

_____
_____
_____
_____
_____

I pace myself so that I am free of stress.   Date

I am comfortable with change.   Date

I love and appreciate myself.   Date

I recognize the power of music, art and beauty in my life.   Date

Weekly Goals

I put my faith into action.   Date

I surround myself with positive, purposeful people.   Date

I speak words of encouragement to myself and others.   Date

I release all expectations and accept the natural flow of my life.   Date

I see opportunity for growth in every situation.   Date

I am inspired.   Date

I maximize my time to maximize my results.   Date

Weekly Goals

Abundance is mine.   Date

I am having the time of my life.   Date

This is my day.   Date

I love my wonderful life.   Date

_____

_____

_____

_____

_____

I release my feelings of tension, anger and frustration.   Date

_____

_____

_____

_____

I practice joy daily.   Date

_____

_____

_____

_____

I am sure of my own worth.   Date

_____

_____

_____

_____

Weekly Goals

_____   _____
_____   _____
_____   _____
_____   _____
_____   _____
_____   _____

I rejoice in the wonder of a new day.   Date
_____
_____
_____
_____
_____

I share my joy with others.   Date
_____
_____
_____
_____
_____

I am honest with myself.   Date
_____
_____
_____
_____
_____

I overcome problems easily.   Date

_____

_____

_____

_____

_____

I reward myself for a job well done.   Date

_____

_____

_____

_____

I love myself more today than I did yesterday. Date

_____

_____

_____

_____

I have the power to change my world.   Date

_____

_____

_____

_____

Meet Judi

Judi doesn't just talk about success... She lives it! In 2003, the US Business Advisory Council named her "Nevada Business Person of the Year" and the Las Vegas Chamber of Commerce awarded her company, Turning Point International, with a "Circle of Excellence" Award. In 1986, the Chamber also honored her as "Woman of Achievement — Entrepreneur."

As an international business leader, Judi knows first hand what it takes to be successful ... especially amidst political, social, and cultural differences. In 1991, she moved to South Africa and became an executive in South Africa's most prestigious media group. Today, she lives in Las Vegas, Nevada and serves as president of Turning Point International, a performance improvement company with offices in Las Vegas and Johannesburg. Her client list reads like a who's who of the world's most prestigious companies and organizations.

Judi served on the Boards of Directors of the Las Vegas Chamber of Commerce Women's Council, the Las Vegas Professional Speakers Association, the World Modeling Association, the International Association of Model Agents, and Women in Communication. The American Women in Radio and Television awarded her their "Outstanding Achievement and Community Service" award.

A speaker of both substance and style, Judi combines her wealth of knowledge and expertise with the inspiration of a motivational speaker and the humor of an entertainer to bring you a program guaranteed to enrich the lives of all who hear her.

"Judi Moreo was a fabulous speaker. She approached what we do every day from a wonderful perspective -- one that we need to hear as a reminder -- listening, confidence, individuality and priorities. Her presentation was engaging, entertaining, and motivating."
> — BECKY NELSON, SYSTEMS DIRECTOR, PROTECTION TECHNOLOGY, ALLSTATE INSURANCE COMPANY

"The response to your talk superceded my wildest expectation. Without exception all delegates verbalized appreciation of your message, but more importantly we have been able to take tangible hints to help improve our overall effectiveness."
> — CLIFF SCLANDERS, SALES MANAGER, DHL WORLDWIDE EXPRESS

"Thank you for sharing your own personal experiences -- I found your examples and stories so easy to imagine and identify with because of the colorful and true-to-life manner in which you shared them with us. I felt like you were a friend to us instead of a lecturer."
> — TAVYN CHALMERS, INVESTEC BANK LIMITED

"Judging by the number of people who came up to talk to you after the General Session, your speech was not only well received, but also stimulated a lot of thinking by attendees prompting the questions. In addition there were many positive responses by attendees noting the very useful and positive comments relative to their own Retail Businesses."
> — RON ROBERTSON, EXECUTIVE VICE PRESIDENT, WESTERN DECORATING PRODUCTS ASSOCIATION

"Thank you for the exciting presentation to our Nurse/Manager group. The group, as a whole, expressed what a terrific presenter you are, and about the enthusiasm and energy they felt at the end of the day."
> — FAYE LINDQUIST, R. N., NURSE MANAGER, PEDIATRICS, McKAY-DEE HOSPITAL CENTER

To book Judi for speaking engagements or to find an event near you, call: 702-896-2228

I feel good about what I have accomplished so far.

The next step toward my goal is easy.

Weekly Goals

_____   _____
_____   _____
_____   _____
_____   _____
_____   _____
_____   _____

I live in unlimited abundance.   Date
_____
_____
_____
_____
_____

I use my free time to my advantage.   Date
_____
_____
_____
_____
_____

My path is straight, my step is sure.   Date
_____
_____
_____
_____
_____

I take myself to new places and observe what happens there.   Date

I show up for life every day.   Date

I treat myself to luxury today.   Date

I am the creator of my life experiences..   Date

Weekly Goals

_____   _____

_____   _____

_____   _____

_____   _____

_____   _____

_____   _____

I let go of my past and embrace my future.   Date

_____

_____

_____

_____

I take responsibility for my attitude.   Date

_____

_____

_____

_____

My passion burns brightly, lighting the path to success.   Date

_____

_____

_____

_____

_____

Now is the most important moment of my life.   Date

I think and speak positively.   Date

I am free of anxiety and stress.   Date

I am confident and enthusiastic.   Date

Balance Wheel

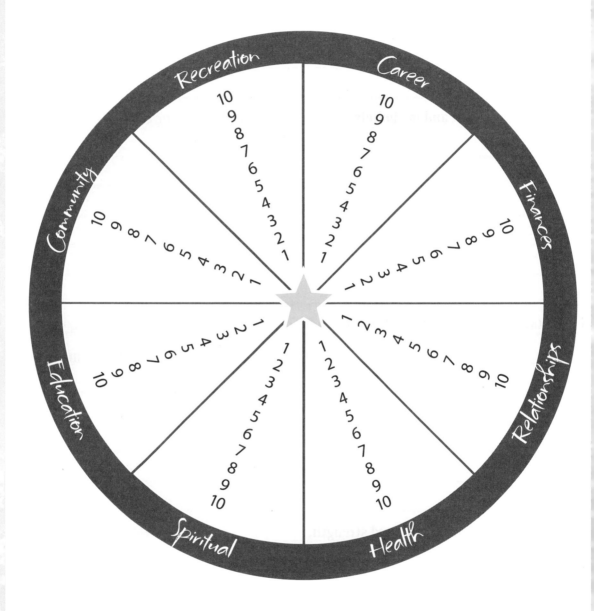

I feel good about what I have accomplished so far.

The next step toward my goal is easy.

Weekly Goals

_____   _____
_____   _____
_____   _____
_____   _____
_____   _____
_____   _____

The sights and sounds of nature inspire me.   Date

I have all the right stuff.   Date

I am an incredible person.   Date

I treat my body with respect.   Date

I am open to new experiences.   Date

My inner voice guides me to make right choices.   Date

Everything I need to succeed is available to me.   Date

Weekly Goals

_____   _____

_____   _____

_____   _____

_____   _____

_____   _____

_____   _____

I am one with the universe.   Date _____

_____

_____

_____

_____

My life is filled with passion and power.   Date _____

_____

_____

_____

_____

I am the perfect person for the job.   Date _____

_____

_____

_____

_____

_____

People respond positively to me.   Date

The answers to all of my questions are within me.   Date

I state my needs clearly.   Date

I awake to the prospect of a wondrous day.   Date

Weekly Goals

_____   _____

_____   _____

_____   _____

_____   _____

_____   _____

_____   _____

Things are going right in my life.   Date

_____

_____

_____

_____

My positive outlook gives me strength.   Date

_____

_____

_____

I respect all living things.   Date

_____

_____

_____

_____

My thoughts and feelings matter.   Date

My life unfolds before me in a beautiful kaleidoscope of color.   Date

My passion for living shatters the limiting bonds of "I should".   Date

There is an artist inside of me.   Date

Balance Wheel

Be aware of wonder. Live a balanced life — learn some and think some and draw and paint and sing and dance and play and work every day some.
—Robert Fulghum

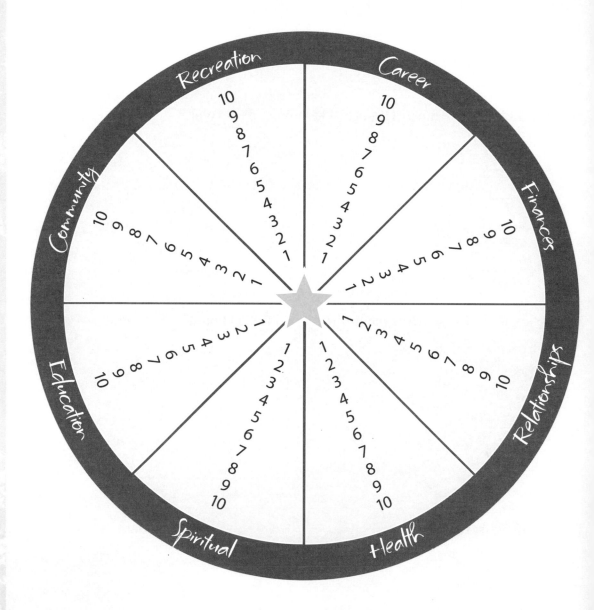

I feel good about what I have accomplished so far.

The next step toward my goal is easy.

Weekly Goals

_____   _____

_____   _____

_____   _____

_____   _____

_____   _____

_____   _____

There is great power in kindness.   Date

_____

_____

_____

_____

Doing what I love brings me health, happiness and prosperity.   Date

_____

_____

_____

_____

I do whatever it takes to achieve the results I desire.   Date

_____

_____

_____

_____

_____

I release any negative thoughts.   Date

My success is multiplying.   Date

I surround myself with loving people.   Date

My eyes are focused on my goal.   Date

Weekly Goals

_____   _____
_____   _____
_____   _____
_____   _____
_____   _____
_____   _____

I take time to rest.   Date

It is OK to express my wants and needs.   Date

My life has a purpose and I know what it is.   Date

My heart is open.   Date

There is always enough.   Date

I think before I speak.   Date

Stress is my past, peace is my present, joy is my future.   Date

Weekly Goals

_____   _____
_____   _____
_____   _____
_____   _____
_____   _____
_____   _____
_____   _____

Miracles surround me.   Date

_____
_____
_____
_____
_____

I am the brightest star in my universe.   Date

_____
_____
_____
_____
_____

My life has order and meaning.   Date

_____
_____
_____
_____
_____

My mind, body and beauty are in perfect balance.   Date

I am showered with wealth.   Date

Fun and laughter are mine to enjoy.   Date

My passion gives birth to my success.   Date

Balance Wheel

Be aware of wonder. Live a balanced life — learn some and think some and draw and paint and sing and dance and play and work every day some.
—Robert Fulghum

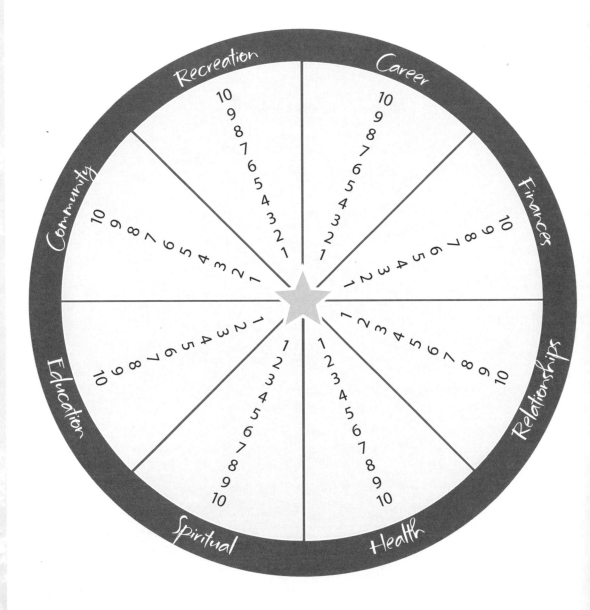

I feel good about what I have accomplished so far.

The next step toward my goal is easy.

Weekly Goals

_____ _____
_____ _____
_____ _____
_____ _____
_____ _____
_____ _____
_____ _____

I am able to express myself clearly.   Date

_____
_____
_____
_____

My mind is alert to possibilities.   Date

_____
_____
_____
_____

My power to achieve grows as my passion ignites.   Date

_____
_____
_____
_____

Success seeks me as I seek success.   Date

The universe conspires with me to bring my dreams to life.   Date

I leap into the graceful flow of my life with enthusiasm.   Date

There is a way even when it seems there isn't.   Date

Weekly Goals

_____   _____
_____   _____
_____   _____
_____   _____
_____   _____
_____   _____

With every breath, I experience the joy and abundance of life.   Date

I am happy and content.   Date

I own my power.   Date

My dreams are coming true.   Date

I trust myself.   Date

My passion gives life to my dreams.   Date

I am organized, disciplined, and focused on my goals.   Date

Weekly Goals

_____   _____
_____   _____
_____   _____
_____   _____
_____   _____
_____   _____

My life is rich and full.   Date
_____
_____
_____
_____
_____

I am on the right track.   Date
_____
_____
_____
_____
_____

I work well with others.   Date
_____
_____
_____
_____
_____

My home is peaceful and filled with love. Date

My life is an adventure. Date

There is something great in store for me. Date

The universe sings perfect harmony to my success. Date

Balance Wheel

Be aware of wonder. Live a balanced life — learn some and think some and draw and paint and sing and dance and play and work every day some.
—Robert Fulghum

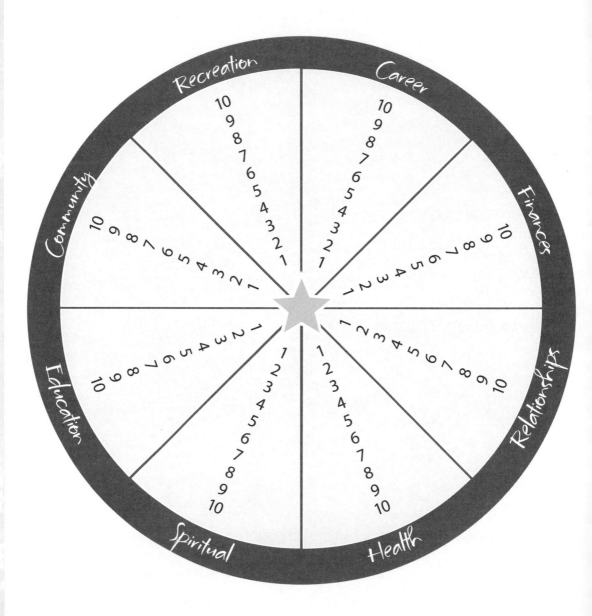

I feel good about what I have accomplished so far.

The next step toward my goal is easy.

Maintaining Momentum

What did I accomplish this year?

What surprised me most about what I was able to do?

How have I changed?

What goals am I continuing to pursue?

What do I want to do next?

There is no crystal ball for the future that we can look into and see with clarity what will transpire in our lives. We must each select our own guiding star and head in that direction in the best way we can at this particular time. Every step we take leads to the next. After a while we look back and see how far we have come.

Some of the steps you will want to include are:

☆ Continue to focus on the positive things that are happening in your life. Don't give any energy to negative thinking. You attract into your life that which you think about.

☆ Give up worry. It is a by-product of fear. When you stay forward focused and have faith, you will no longer need to carry either worry or fear with you.

☆ Realize what a unique individual you are. There's no one in the universe exactly like you. You are one of a kind. You have your own special talents, abilities and skills.

☆ Count your blessings every day. Did you eat today? Do you have shelter and a warm bed in which to sleep? Are you in good health? Do you have family and friends? Do you live in a country where you can express your thoughts and opinions?

☆ Give up anger, blame, grudges, resentment, and self-pity. Find fault with no one.

☆ Give up comparison, judgment, and condemnation. Learn to forgive others.

☆ Forgive yourself as well. You are and always have been doing the best you can. If you have made mistakes along the way, learn from them and put them behind you. After all, you are human.

☆ Continue to find something to appreciate in everyone you meet, in everything you do, and for everything you receive.

When we truly understand that we have the ability to create the kind of life we want to live, we will create a life of purpose, passion, and power. You are more than enough!

21 things to do before I die

1.

2.

3.

4.

5.

6.

7.

8.

9.

10.

11.

12.

13.

14.

15.

16.

17.

18.

19.

20.

21.

Beattie, Melody. *Beyond Codependency*. New York: Harper/Hazelden, 1983.

Beattie, Melody. *Codependent No More*. New York: Harper/Hazelden, 1987.

Branden, Nathaniel. *The Psychology of Self-Esteem*. New York: Bantam Books, 1987.

Branden, Nathaniel. *How to Raise Your Self-Esteem*. New York: Bantam Books, 1987.

Bristol, Claude M. *The Magic of Believing*. New York: Pocket Books, 1991.

Carter-Scott, Cherie, Fiona Carmichael, Judi Moreo. *Ordinary Women, Extraordinary Success*. Franklin Lakes, New Jersey: Career Press, 2002.

Dyer, Dr. Wayne. *Gifts from Eykis*. New York: Pocket Books, 1984.

Ferrell, Jesse. *How You Leave Them Feeling*. Las Vegas, Nevada: Jess Talk Speaking Services, LLC, 2006

Frankl, Victor E. *Man's Search for Meaning*. New York: Pocket Books, 1963.

Freston, Kathy. *Expect A Miracle*. New York: St. Martin's Griffin, 2003.

Hill, Napoleon. *Think and Grow Rich*. San Diego: Aventine Press, 2004.

Jay, Robin. *The Art of the Business Lunch*. Franklin Lakes, New Jersey: Career Press, 2004.

Klein, Allen. *The Healing Power of Humor*. Los Angeles: Jeremy P. Tarcher, 1989.

Kusher, Harold S. *When Bad Things Happen to Good People*. New York: Avon Publishers, 1989.

Mandino, Og. *The Greatest Salesman in the World*. New York: Bantam Books, 1983.

Mandino, Og. *University of Success*. New York: Bantam Books, 1982.

Moreo, Judi, and Fiona Carmichael, *Conquer the Brain Drain: 52 Creative Ways to Pump Up Productivity*, Kansas City, Kansas, National Press Publications, 2002.

Moreo, Judi. *You Are More Than Enough: Every Woman's Guide to Purpose, Passion & Power*. Las Vegas: Stephen's Press, 2007.

RoAne, Susan. *How to Work a Room*. New York: Shapolsky Publishers, Inc., 1988.

Schuller, Dr. Robert. *The Be (Happy) Attitudes*. Waco, Texas: Word Books, 1985.

Schuller, Dr. Robert. *Tough Minded Faith for Tender Hearted People*. New York: Bantam Books, 1985.

Seabury, David. *The Art of Self-ishness*. New York: Pocket Books, 1964.

Wilkinson, Bruce, David Kopp and Heather Kopp. *The Dream Giver*. Sisters, Oregon: Multnomah Publishers, 2003.

Wilkinson, Bruce. *The Prayer of Jabez*. Sisters, Oregon: Multnomah Publishers, 2000.